Visual Geography Series®

# PORTUGAL

## ...in Pictures

Prepared by
**Geography Department**

**Lerner Publications Company**
Minneapolis

Independent Picture Service

**Fishermen dry and mend their nets along the beach at Nazaré, a western town midway along Portugal's Atlantic coast.**

This book is an all-new edition in the Visual Geography Series. Previous editions were published by Sterling Publishing Company, New York City. The text, set in 10/12 Century Textbook, is fully revised and updated, and new photographs, maps, charts, and captions have been added.

LIBRARY OF CONGRESS CATALOGING-IN-PUBLICATION DATA

Portugal in pictures / prepared by Geography Department, Lerner Publications Company.
    p. cm. — (Visual geography series)
    Rev. ed. of: Portugal in pictures / prepared by James Nach.
    Includes index.
    Summary: Introduces the land, history, government, people, and economy of the small country on the western side of the Iberian peninsula.
    ISBN 0-8225-1886-4 (lib. bdg.)
    1. Portugal. [1. Portugal.]  I. Nach, James, Portugal in pictures.  II. Lerner Publications Company. Geography Department.  III. Series: Visual geography series (Minneapolis, Minn.)
DP517.P633   1991
946.9—dc20                                    90-26919

International Standard Book Number: 0-8225-1886-4
Library of Congress Catalog Card Number: 90-26919

## VISUAL GEOGRAPHY SERIES®

**Publisher**
Harry Jonas Lerner
**Associate Publisher**
Nancy M. Campbell
**Senior Editor**
Mary M. Rodgers
**Editors**
Gretchen Bratvold
Dan Filbin
Tom Streissguth
**Photo Researcher**
Kerstin Coyle
**Editorial/Photo Assistants**
Marybeth Campbell
Colleen Sexton
**Consultants/Contributors**
Ellen W. Sapega
Sandra K. Davis
**Designer**
Jim Simondet
**Cartographer**
Carol F. Barrett
**Indexers**
Kristine S. Schubert
Sylvia Timian
**Production Manager**
Gary J. Hansen

Independent Picture Service

**A Portuguese artisan arranges blocks of cement to form a mosaic pavement.**

**Acknowledgments**

Title page photo by Dr. Roma Hoff.

Elevation contours adapted from *The Times Atlas of the World,* seventh comprehensive edition (New York: Times Books, 1985).

Manufactured in the United States of America
2 3 4 5 6 7 8 9 10 – JR – 00 99 98 97 96

Pena Castle dominates a mountain east of the Portuguese capital of Lisbon. Built on the ruins of a sixteenth-century monastery, the nineteenth-century castle exhibits a variety of architectural styles.

# Contents

## AZORES ISLANDS

CORVO I.

FLORES I.

SÃO JORGE I.

FAIAL I.

PICO I.

TERCEIRA I.

SÃO MIGUEL I.

SANTA MARIA I.

| 0 | 50 | 100 Miles |
| 0 | 50 | 100 Kilometers |

*NORTH ATLANTIC OCEAN*

## MADEIRA ISLANDS

MADEIRA I.

Funchal

| 0 | 50 Miles |
| 0 | 50 Kilometers |

Minho R.

Bragança

Braga

Vila do Conde

Matozinhos

Oporto

Douro R.

Aveiro

Mondego R.

Coimbra
CONIMBRIGA
(Ruins)

Castelo
Branco

Nazaré

Fátima

Aljubarrota

Tomar

Tejo R.

SPAIN

Peniche

Santarém

Mérida

Vila Franca
de Xira

Sintra
Colares

Estoril

LISBON

Estremoz

Setúbal

Évora

Bay of
Setúbal

Sado R.

Sines

Beja

Guadiana R.

CAPE ST. VINCENT

Lagos

Sagres

Faro

Olhão

*Gulf of Cádiz*

## PORTUGAL

N
↑

——— Administrative Boundaries

——— Major Roads

| 0 | 50 | 100 Miles |
| 0 | 50 | 100 Kilometers |

60°

20°

0°

20°

Arctic Circle

*NORWEGIAN SEA*

EUROPE
PORTUGAL

| 0 | 400 Miles |
| 0 | 400 Kilometers |

*NORTH ATLANTIC OCEAN*

60°

20°

40°

*MEDITERRANEAN SE*

### METRIC CONVERSION CHART
To Find Approximate Equivalents

| WHEN YOU KNOW: | MULTIPLY BY: | TO FIND: |
|---|---|---|
| **AREA** | | |
| acres | 0.41 | hectares |
| square miles | 2.59 | square kilometers |
| **CAPACITY** | | |
| gallons | 3.79 | liters |
| **LENGTH** | | |
| feet | 30.48 | centimeters |
| yards | 0.91 | meters |
| miles | 1.61 | kilometers |
| **MASS** (weight) | | |
| pounds | 0.45 | kilograms |
| tons | 0.91 | metric tons |
| **VOLUME** | | |
| cubic yards | 0.77 | cubic meters |
| **TEMPERATURE** | | |
| degrees Fahrenheit | 0.56 (*after* subtracting 32) | degrees Celsius |

Using a craggy rock as a platform, boys dive into the sparkling waters of the Atlantic Ocean in southern Portugal.

# Introduction

Lying along the Atlantic Ocean in southwesternmost Europe, Portugal has long turned its back on the continent and has faced the sea. For centuries, the country survived and thrived because it used the oceans for fishing and exploration. Portugal's long coastline has also given invaders, traders, and visitors easy access to its shores.

The Romans controlled Portugal, which they called Lusitania, from the first century B.C. to the fifth century A.D. After that time, Portuguese territory was a target for conquest by Germanic and Arab peoples. By the twelfth century, however, northern Portugal had become an independent kingdom. A century later, southern Portugal was able to join this realm.

After establishing peace within Portugal, the country's kings and princes turned toward the sea for adventure and trade. In the 1400s and 1500s, Portuguese explorers charted the way to Africa, India, and Asia. They brought back spices, silks, and precious stones that merchants sold for large profits in European markets. Expanding trade led to the founding of colonies, and Portugal became the hub of a vast empire that stretched from Brazil in South America to China in Asia.

Despite its worldwide activities, Portugal changed little over the next several centuries. Its domestic economy depended almost entirely on agriculture. In the north, farmers grew grapevines and raised livestock on small plots. Southern landholders operated large estates that produced grain, olives, and cork. Most of the country's income came from its colonies, and without colonial imports and exports Portugal would have been very poor.

**Grape pickers bring their baskets filled with fruit to wine-making centers in the Douro River Valley. This area of northern Portugal has long produced port wine, one of the nation's main exports.**

**Women in northern Portugal discuss the price of cheese at a local market.**

In the early nineteenth century, Portugal's wealthiest colony—Brazil—declared its independence. This loss made Portugal more reliant on its African and Asian territories, which still provided raw materials and markets for Portuguese goods. Further changes occurred in the early twentieth century, when public unrest and political chaos within Portugal toppled its monarchy. By 1926 a dictatorship had replaced the king and royal government.

For nearly 50 years, António de Oliveira Salazar ruled Portugal. Censorship was strict, and political opposition was not allowed. Salazar's regime did little to develop agriculture and industry, both of which suffered a long decline. In the 1960s and 1970s, Portugal's colonies revolted to gain their independence. By the mid-1970s, even the Portuguese army was ready for change, and it staged a revolution in 1974.

Surrounded by army officers, General António de Spínola delivered a speech in May 1974, after taking office as president of Portugal. A military overthrow a month earlier had ended the long dictatorship of António de Oliveira Salazar and of his successor, Marcello Caetano.

During the first decade after the revolution, Portugal tried a variety of political and economic strategies to solve its many problems. It gave up its African and Asian colonies, for example, and turned toward Europe for investment and guidance. In 1986 Portugal joined the European Community (now called the European Union—EU), an economic association to which most western European nations belong. Together EU members make trade policies that benefit the entire group.

The EU has invested large amounts of money in Portugal, which is the association's poorest nation. Many Portuguese hope that these funds will modernize agriculture and industry. Other Portuguese look back with nostalgia at their country's past and wonder if their nation can survive while competing with the bigger and richer states in the EU. These conflicting attitudes reflect Portugal's uncertain future.

In recent years, Portugal has used foreign funds to improve its overland transportation network. This highway runs near Vila Franca de Xira, a town in western Portugal that is famous for its bullfights.

7

White beaches and greenish blue waters draw sunbathers and swimmers to Lagos in the Algarve—the southernmost region of Portugal.

# 1) The Land

Located in southwestern Europe, the Republic of Portugal covers 35,553 square miles—an area about the size of the state of Indiana. The North Atlantic Ocean laps against the country's long western coast. The Gulf of Cádiz, which leads to the Mediterranean Sea, lies to the south. Portugal shares its northern and eastern land boundaries with Spain, and together these two nations occupy the Iberian Peninsula. Two island groups in the North Atlantic Ocean —the Azores and the Madeiras—are also Portuguese territory.

## Topography

Rectangular in shape, mainland Portugal stretches for 350 miles from north to south and is 125 miles across at its widest point. The country has many different surface features. The land slopes from northeast to southwest and contains low plains broken by mountains. The plains belong to a large plateau called the Meseta, which covers most of Spain and part of eastern Portugal. The Madeiras and the Azores are volcanic island groups that differ from the mainland and from each other in terrain and economic activities.

### THE MAINLAND

Northern Portugal's parallel mountain ranges are extensions of the Cantabrian Mountains of northwestern Spain. In Por-

tugal, these mountains average 1,000 feet in height but in some places rise to 3,200 feet above sea level. Among the chains are narrow valleys, where farmers grow crops on small acreages. Centuries ago, workers in the northeast cut terraces, or steps, into the mountainsides to create level fields. The terraced fields still yield grapes for the making of port wine and *vinhos verdes* (meaning "green wines").

The coastal plain in northern Portugal is very narrow. In the south, however, it

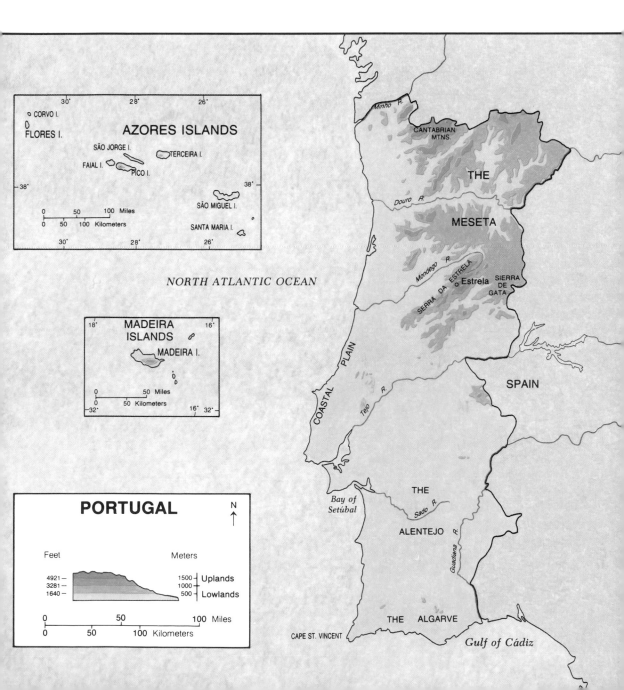

Farmers have carved terraces (tiered fields) into a hillside in the Douro Valley to increase the amount of land available for agriculture.

reaches 30 miles in width and contains salt marshes and broad sand dunes. Mountains again dominate the landscape in central Portugal, where the Serra da Estrela, the country's tallest chain, begins. It contains Estrela, which, at 6,532 feet, is the nation's highest point. Another range, the Sierra de Gata, rises in Spain and extends into east central Portugal.

Southern Portugal's Atlantic coast, where farming and fishing are common occupations, has fertile soil and a mild climate. In the south, gently rolling hills cover inland regions called the Alentejo. Many of Portugal's largest and most productive farms are found in this area.

Situated in the extreme south of Portugal is the Algarve, the hottest, driest re-

The breaking waves of the Atlantic Ocean have shaped rocky headlands along the west central Portuguese coast near the fishing town of Peniche.

In many parts of Portugal, farmers still use windmills to grind grain and to bring water to their land.

Courtesy of Minneapolis Public Library and Information Center

gion in the country. The Algarve has a similar climate to North Africa, which lies 140 miles away. Within the Algarve is Cape St. Vincent, the southwesternmost point on the European continent.

### THE MADEIRAS AND THE AZORES

The Madeiras are located in the North Atlantic about 535 miles southwest of the Portuguese capital of Lisbon and 350 miles off the northwestern coast of Africa. The group consists of two large islands and several uninhabited islets. Most of the population of 253,800 live on the main island of Madeira, which has jagged volcanic ridges and fertile valleys. At one time, thick forests covered much of the island, but settlers cut or burned most of these

Independent Picture Service

Large acreages of wheat thrive in the Alentejo during the summer months. Irrigation Is necessary to produce crops in this dry area of southern Portugal.

11

Courtesy of Catherine F. Rodgers

From a distance, the island of Flores—one of the Azores—is a patchwork of terraced fields and woodlands. Portugal has governed these islands in the North Atlantic Ocean since their discovery in the 1400s. The nation also has authority over the Madeiras, an island group that lies off the western coast of Africa.

woodlands for farms or lumber. Madeira's warm climate is ideal for growing grapes and sugarcane. The grapes produce a famous sweet red wine called Madeira.

Hilly and wooded, the Azores are a group of nine major islands and several smaller islets that lie about 1,000 miles west of Lisbon in the North Atlantic Ocean. Many of the 237,800 inhabitants are farmers who raise grain, vegetables, pineapples, oranges, tea, and tobacco in the islands' rich volcanic soil. In recent years, the Azores have gained importance as a crossroads of air routes and undersea telegraph cables between Europe and North America. The islands also serve as an air base for U.S. and European military planes flying to the Middle East and Africa.

## Rivers

All of Portugal's longest rivers begin in Spain, and some form the border between these two countries on the Iberian Peninsula. From north to south, the most important rivers are the Minho, the Douro, the Tejo, and the Guadiana. Shorter waterways, such as the Mondego and the Sado, lie entirely within Portugal.

The Minho, Portugal's northernmost river, also runs through northwestern Spain. The waterway forms about 45 miles of the Portuguese-Spanish border before emptying into the Atlantic Ocean. The nation's chief northern river is the Douro, which flows for a total of 584 miles toward its outlet on the Atlantic at the city of Oporto. Winding through the wine-making

Courtesy of August Sepega

The **Douro River** flows through northern Portugal as well as northern Spain. Farmers have long used the river's steep banks for growing grapes.

Courtesy of Transinsular, S. A.

**Container ships berth at Lisbon's extensive dock facilities on the Tejo River.**

country of northern Portugal, the Douro has steep banks into which farmers have cut terraces for growing grapes. Engineers have built dams at several points along the river to generate hydroelectric power.

Running for more than 600 miles, the Tejo River is the longest waterway on the Iberian Peninsula and divides Portugal nearly in half. The river crosses Portugal for about 140 miles before reaching the Atlantic Ocean. As it nears the sea, the Tejo becomes an estuary (a place where the river meets the sea) and forms a fine natural harbor. Lisbon, Portugal's chief seaport, developed along the northern bank of this estuary.

Southern Portugal's principal river is the Guadiana, which marks the border with Spain at two separate places. About half

In the resort town of Vila do Conde, people pile dried cod-fish onto wheelbarrows for transport to market. Cod are an important Atlantic catch for Portuguese fishermen.

of the river's total length of 340 miles touches or flows through Portuguese territory before emptying into the Gulf of Cádiz.

## Flora and Fauna

Portugal is home to many types of vegetation. Stands of pine and oak grow north of the Tejo River, where rainfall is plentiful. Olive trees, whose fruit supplies a valuable oil, thrive in the drier soil south of the Tejo. Cork oak trees flourish in the south, and their bark provides cork—the raw material for 80 percent of the bottle stoppers used around the world. Sailors have brought several kinds of non-native trees, such as the eucalyptus, to Portugal from foreign countries.

Portugal's forests provide habitats for many animals. Lynx are common in central inland areas, and wild boars thrive in the forests of the Algarve. Remote moun-

Cork oak trees are green throughout the year. In summer, harvesters cut long, narrow strips off the outer bark, being careful to avoid the inner layers. Over time, these inner layers continue to build up, providing future cork supplies.

tain areas also contain boars, as well as wolves, deer, goats, and foxes. Portugal's rivers teem with fish, including carp, trout, and salmon, and the Atlantic Ocean yields large quantities of sardines and tuna.

A wide variety of small animals and birds lives in the country's forested regions, but hunting has greatly reduced their numbers. Quail, ducks, and pheasant are popular game birds. Rugged and underdeveloped, northern Portugal shelters many species of rare or endangered birds, including golden eagles, black storks, and griffon vultures. Many of these birds nest in cliffs throughout the region.

## Climate

Portugal's long Atlantic coast feels the full effect of a warm air current called the North Atlantic Drift. It is a branch of the Gulf Stream Current that swirls northeastward from the Caribbean Sea. The North Atlantic Drift warms winds blowing off the Atlantic Ocean. These breezes give most of Portugal a subtropical climate, with long, dry summers and mild, slightly wet winters.

In the nation's two largest cities—Lisbon and Oporto—the average temperature is about 50 °F in January, the coldest month, and varies between 75 ° and 85 °F in July, the hottest month. Cool ocean breezes make summer temperatures on the coasts pleasant, and in winter snow rarely falls, except in the mountains. The plains and coasts of southern Portugal have hot summers and dry winters.

Annual rainfall in Portugal varies from region to region. Most of the precipitation occurs in November and December. Summers bring little rain. Mountainous areas receive more rainfall than the lowlands do. Up to 110 inches of rain and snow fall each year in the Serra da Estrela. In the north, the average annual precipitation is about 60 inches, but it tapers off to about 30 inches per year in southern Portugal.

Courtesy of Minneapolis Public Library and Information Center

**Portugal has a warm, sunny climate in the summer, when visitors and Portuguese flock to the nation's many beaches. Some of the beaches have become badly polluted in recent years, and a program to clean them up is under way.**

Workers guide donkeys loaded with cork to a processing center. Portugal's cork oaks provide the raw material for most of the world's bottle stoppers, bulletin boards, and fishing-pole handles.

## Natural Resources

Although Portugal has some minerals, its mining industry is not well developed. Mountainous areas contain substantial amounts of wolframite, which can be made into tungsten—a strong metal. Scientists have found veins of coal in the north and deposits of copper in the south. Small quantities of tin, gold, and uranium (used in nuclear power plants to produce energy) also exist.

Forests cover about one-third of Portugal's land and have long been harvested for use in the building and manufacturing industries. To replant cleared land, the government often chooses pine trees, which resist strong winds, grow rapidly, and can live in thin or dry soils. Cork bark stripped from evergreen oak trees brings in substantial revenue.

Portugal's rivers, particularly the Tejo and Douro, are major sources of hydropower for the country. The Atlantic Ocean provides Portuguese fishermen with seafood. In recent years, however, catches have declined as overfishing has depleted the Atlantic's fish population.

## Cities

Compared with most European nations, Portugal's population—9.9 million—is small. More than thirty percent of the people live in urban areas, mainly in Lisbon and Oporto. Many of the country's inhabitants reside in farming and fishing villages that lie near midsize market towns.

### LISBON

Located on the Atlantic coast, Lisbon is Portugal's capital, largest city, and principal port. About 681,000 people live within Lisbon's city limits, and 1.9 million reside in its metropolitan area. Built on a series of hills, Lisbon displays old and new architectural designs. In the central part of the city, modern buildings face broad, eighteenth-century plazas. Some of these areas were damaged during a fire in 1988.

During its long history, Lisbon has been the point of arrival for many conquerors. Roman soldiers and Moorish invaders from North Africa occupied the site. In the 1100s, the Portuguese recaptured the city from the Moors, and it became the nation's official capital about 150 years later.

In the fifteenth and sixteenth centuries—Portugal's main era of exploration and colonization—adventurers sailed from Lisbon's docks to lands throughout the world. The city became the headquarters of a vast overseas empire. In 1755 an earthquake leveled Lisbon, and a tidal wave and fire following the quake did further damage. Many of the city's structures date from the eighteenth and nineteenth centuries, when the capital was rebuilt.

Since World War II (1939–1945), Lisbon has expanded its harbor to include oil-refining and storage areas, shipbuilding and repair stations, and other industrial complexes. Many of Portugal's manufactured goods leave the country from the port of Lisbon.

Lisbon, Portugal's capital and largest city, sits on a series of hills on the banks of the Tejo River. Some of the crumbling pastel-and-white buildings in the oldest parts of Lisbon are being restored. The city—despite its size, modernized docks, and expanding economic activities—still has a quiet and unhurried atmosphere.

**17**

Called Portus Cale in Roman times, Oporto lies on the banks of the Douro River and is the most important port and industrial center in northern Portugal. The country's second largest city, Oporto has a population of more than 309,500, and 1.7 million people live in its metropolitan area.

Since the 1700s, the city's trade with British wine merchants has made it a center for the production and transportation of port wine. About 80 wine-storage buildings line the banks of the Douro River. In addition, Oporto has factories that process food, that refine oil, and that make textiles, tires, and ceramics.

The port of Setúbal (population 103,240) lies on a peninsula south of Lisbon. Setúbal has access to the protected Bay of Setúbal, into which the Sado River flows. A bridge completed in 1966 links the peninsula with the capital, enabling Setúbal to develop several important industries. Its shipbuilding facilities, fish-canning factories, and other enterprises are busy year-round. Brightly painted fishing trawlers arrive at the city's docks each morning, bringing catches to sell at the local fish auction.

Coimbra (population 147,700), situated on the Mondego River in west central Portugal, has a long and colorful past. Founded by the Romans, the city was occupied by the Moors until the eleventh century. It was the capital of Portugal in the twelfth and thirteenth centuries, as well as the seat of power of a Roman Catholic bishop. Coimbra contains the nation's oldest university, several important libraries, and fine museums. Historic religious buildings are scattered throughout the city. Many small industries employ local people.

Photo © Tony Arruza

Oporto's granite houses and large wine-storage facilities line both banks of the Douro River.

Small, brightly painted fishing boats bring their catches into the port of Setúbal.

Located on the Mondego River, Coimbra is a lively university town that also serves as a farming hub for central Portugal.

Beginning in the second century B.C., Portugal was under the control of the Roman Empire, which was centered in southern Italy. The largest Roman ruins in Portugal lie south of Coimbra at Conimbriga. The site includes baths, courtyards, mosaic floors, and defensive walls. Archaeologists have excavated only a small portion of the estimated 32 acres of ruins.

# 2) History and Government

Portugal shares much of its early history with Spain. Some ancient states covered territories that have since been divided between the two nations. Artifacts suggest that people have lived on the Iberian Peninsula for many thousands of years. Ancient burial mounds that contain pottery and weaponry have been found in many parts of western Portugal.

Portugal's first recorded inhabitants were the Iberians, who came to the region about 5,000 years ago from North Africa or the eastern Mediterranean. Not long after their arrival, the Iberians began to split into smaller groups that spread throughout Portugal. North of the Douro River, for example, lived herders and farmers who were called Galicians. The Lusitanians, another Iberian subgroup, occupied the area between the Douro and Tejo rivers.

Fierce and warlike, the Lusitanians defended their villages against attacks by other Iberians. After about 900 B.C., the Lusitanians came into contact with Celts from northern Europe, who were migrating to various regions of the continent. The newcomers shared their knowledge of met-

20

alwork and introduced better methods of raising livestock. For several hundred years, the Celts and the Lusitanians intermarried and had little contact with outsiders.

## Early Conquerors

In the third century B.C., traders and soldiers arrived in Portugal from Carthage, the capital of an important commercial nation in North Africa. The newcomers established outposts along the southern seacoast and exchanged goods with local inhabitants. Eventually, the traders occupied the coastal area.

The Carthaginians made few stops in northern Portugal, except to hire Lusitanians to fight under the Carthaginian general Hannibal. He was battling the Roman Republic for control of trade throughout the Mediterranean. In 218 B.C., Hannibal and his forces crossed what are now Spain and France to reach the Roman army in Italy. After Hannibal's defeat in 201 B.C., Carthage lost the Iberian Peninsula to the Romans.

### ROMAN RULE

Roman soldiers seized southern Portugal, where trade with Europe was already well established. Accustomed to foreign influences, the people of the south easily accepted Roman rule. In northern Portugal, however, many battles and defeats slowed the Roman conquest. In the second century B.C., the Romans went north to fight the Lusitanians, who rallied around a local leader named Viriathus. His hit-and-run tactics frustrated Roman advances for a time, but the murder of Viriathus in 139 B.C. weakened local resistance to Roman authority.

By the first century B.C., the Roman army had finally subdued the Iberian Peninsula and had set up a government. The Romans established or enlarged many ports and military towns in the new territory, including Portus Cale (Oporto), Olisipo (Lis-

bon), and Bracara Augusta (Braga). The new government laid roads, staked out large farming estates, and put Roman laws into place. The region's people adopted Latin (the Roman language), dressed in Roman styles, and began to accept Roman customs. Many of the local inhabitants accepted the gods of the Roman religion.

In 27 B.C., the Romans divided the Iberian Peninsula into three provinces. Most of what is now Portugal was included in the province of Lusitania, with its capital at Augusta Emerita (now Mérida, Spain). By the fourth century A.D., missionaries had brought Christianity, a one-god religion, to Lusitania. This Christian faith (later called Roman Catholicism) had arisen in the eastern part of the Roman Empire and eventually became the empire's official religion. In Lusitania, Catholic bishops established headquarters in Ossonoba (now Faro) and Augusta Emerita.

Photo by Claude E. Leroy

**The remains of a Roman-era temple stand in Évora, an old city in south central Portugal. The ruins date to about the third century A.D., when Roman religious beliefs, which honored many gods, were still in place. Eventually, the Roman Empire adopted the one-god Christian faith.**

Rome continued to rule Lusitania until the fifth century, when various Germanic peoples attacked the Iberian Peninsula. Each of the conquering groups occupied a separate territory. The Alans, for example, took over Lusitania, and the Suevi invaded Galicia. The Vandals seized land in southern Portugal and southern Spain.

None of these peoples held its territory for long. The Suevi captured the lands of the Alans and the Vandals in the mid-sixth century. Soon afterward, another group of Germanic invaders—called the Visigoths—challenged the Suevi and by 585 had added the Suevi kingdom to an expanding Visigothic state. The Visigoths held most of the former Roman provinces on the Iberian Peninsula and ruled them according to Germanic laws. Visigothic kings were elected, for example, and did not inherit their office. The elections fostered the growth of rival factions that competed for power in the sixth and seventh centuries.

# The Moors

In the early 700s, members of the Witiza—a dissatisfied Visigothic faction—invited skilled soldiers from North Africa to participate in a revolt against King Roderick, the ruler of the Visigoths. The recruits were a mixture of Arab and Berber peoples known as Moors. They had adopted a new one-god religion called Islam, which had arisen in Arabia. The religion's followers were known as Muslims.

The Muslim invasion of the Iberian Peninsula began in Spain in 711. The Moors scattered Roderick's forces and killed him in battle. Rather than returning to North Africa, the invaders went on to take the wealthy cities of Córdoba and Toledo (both now in Spain). The Witiza faction, which had sought only Roderick's defeat, could not prevent the Moorish conquest of other parts of the peninsula. By the mid-eighth century, the Moors controlled all but the mountainous areas of the northern Iberian Peninsula.

Photo by Bettmann Archive

**The Vandals, a Germanic people from northern Europe, seized Roman-held territory in Portugal in the early fifth century.**

Photo © Tony Aruzza

**The architecture of the Alentejo has been heavily influenced by Moorish styles. The Moors, who originated in North Africa, conquered southern Portugal in the eighth century.**

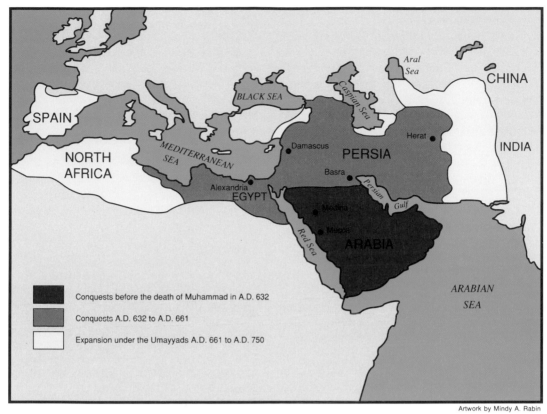

Artwork by Mindy A. Rabin

The Moorish takeover was part of a much larger expansion effort that also affected sections of Asia and Africa. The Moors followed the Islamic faith, which a leader named Muhammad had founded in Arabia. The westernmost land under Islamic control—in southern Portugal—was called al-Gharb (the west) in Arabic. This region is now known as the Algarve.

Catholic nobles in northern Portugal resisted the Muslim Moors. Within 50 years of the Arab invasion, Christian forces had driven the Moors south of the Douro River and had recovered the land surrounding the city of Portus Cale. By the mid-eleventh century, the Christians had extended their territory southward to Coimbra. The nobles reorganized the Christian lands, which included large sections of northern Spain. The areas around Portus Cale and Coimbra became counties within Galicia, a domain that belonged to the northern Iberian kingdom called León-Castile.

### MOORISH RULE

During the centuries of Arab occupation, most Moors lived south of the Tejo River—in the Alentejo and the Algarve—where the climate resembled that of their North African homeland. The Moors controlled what had been large Roman estates or dwelled in Roman-built cities. For the most part, the conquerors were content to be overlords, using local people as administrators and tax collectors whenever possible.

Although some Iberians adopted Islam, much of the population in southern Portugal remained Roman Catholic. Jews, who had arrived from other Muslim-held lands, were also free to practice their religion. The Moors allowed urban Jewish people—many of whom were traders, artists, and scholars—to follow their professions. The mix of Moorish and Christian traditions influenced architecture, decoration, and other arts. The Moors also supported education, and Christian, Muslim, and Jewish scholarship flourished during the period.

Events in Islamic lands in Africa and Asia affected the Moors on the Iberian Peninsula. Moorish rulers, called caliphs, often left the peninsula in the hands of local governors and returned to Africa to deal with splits in the Islamic leadership. In the absence of the caliphs, Moorish control sometimes faltered. At other times, powerful caliphs increased Moorish authority by bringing in fresh troops and strengthening the peninsula's defenses.

## Afonso Henriques and the Fight for Independence

Continual fighting between Christian and Muslim armies shifted the boundaries between Christian and Muslim lands for several hundred years. Records from the mid-eleventh century refer to Portugal as the Christian county of Portucale located between the Minho and Tejo rivers. In 1096 the king of León-Castile, Alfonso VI, made Portucale semi-independent. He gave the territory to his French son-in-law Henry of Burgundy, who strengthened the power of the Roman Catholic Church in his domain. Henry brought in French monks to run the religious districts of Braga and Coimbra.

When Henry died in 1112, Portugal passed to his widow, Teresa, the daughter of Alfonso VI. She angered Portuguese nobles by granting considerable power to her father's friends. Her son Prince Afonso Henriques led Portuguese nobles in a revolt that defeated Teresa's army in 1128. Although in control of Portucale, Afonso Henriques still was under the authority of his cousin Alfonso VII, the new king of León-Castile.

Seeking greater independence, Prince Afonso Henriques fought Alfonso VII for about 10 years. But the prince put aside this war in the late 1130s, when he saw a chance to win territory from the Moors.

Courtesy of D. G. C. S.

Born in about 1109, Afonso Henriques spent much of his adult life fighting battles both against his relatives and against the Moors. He claimed the kingship of Portugal in 1139. His Spanish cousin recognized this claim in 1143, and Afonso Henriques earned the Roman Catholic pope's approval in 1172.

Photo by Mansell Collection

With the help of foreign Christian soldiers, Afonso Henriques successfully attacked Moorish strongholds in Lisbon, Santarém, Beja, and Évora in the twelfth century.

By then, power struggles among the Moors had divided their lands into separate holdings called *taifas*. This change weakened Arab control of southern Portugal.

Afonso Henriques successfully attacked Santarém and Lisbon in the 1140s. After these victories, Muslim leaders were forced to pay the prince money and goods as tribute. The Moors moved the border of their lands from the Tejo River almost to the Algarve in southernmost Portugal.

These triumphs and payments further empowered the prince, who referred to himself as Afonso I, king of Portugal, beginning in 1139. At a meeting in 1143, Alfonso VII formally recognized the claim of Afonso I in exchange for promises of future military help. This event established the Portuguese Afonsine dynasty (family of rulers).

Independent Picture Service

In the 1200s and 1300s, Portugal began to expand its shipbuilding industry.

By the mid-twelfth century, Portugal was an independent country with its capital at Coimbra. The Moors, however, remained a threat to the realm. Battles with the Muslims continued throughout Afonso's reign, which ended in 1185. He was succeeded by his son, Sancho I, who fought the Moors and encouraged the growth of trade and agriculture.

## Portugal Grows and Develops

Early Portuguese kings knew that their rule became stronger when they had the support of the Roman Catholic Church and rich landowners. In 1211, to strengthen the cooperation among these groups, the new king, Afonso II, assembled high-ranking clergy and nobles at Coimbra. This first meeting evolved into the *cortes,* or royal Portuguese parliament.

During the reigns of Afonso II and his successor, Sancho II, the church and the kings competed for land, income, and authority. As a result of this friction, the Roman Catholic pope denied Sancho II's claim to the throne in 1245, and the kingship passed to Sancho's brother Afonso III.

Under Afonso III, Portugal expanded to its present size after royal forces pushed the Moors from the Algarve—the last Moorish territory on the Portuguese side of the peninsula. Afonso III also assembled a cortes in 1253 in which, for the first time, merchants and townspeople were allowed to attend along with the clergy and the nobles.

Portugal flourished during the long reign of Afonso III's son Dinis (1279–1325), who founded the kingdom's first university, developed agriculture, and fostered shipbuilding. Fishing and trading became well established, and cargoes of foreign metals, weapons, and textiles began to arrive in Lisbon. Ships filled with Portuguese wine, wax, honey, and olive oil left the city for ports in northern Europe. Lisbon's wealth and importance made it a natural choice as a new capital, and by

As economic activities progressed in Lisbon *(left)*, it soon became more important than Coimbra, the country's ancient capital. By the late thirteenth century, the royal government operated from Lisbon.

1298 the government was moved to Lisbon from Coimbra.

In the 1340s, rats on ships docking in Lisbon brought a deadly disease called the Black Death into Portugal. The plague swept through the Portuguese population, killing one out of every three citizens. A lack of workers weakened the once-productive farming estates. In the next few decades, the government responded to this crisis by seizing all idle land and arranging for it to be replanted.

## A New Dynasty

Portugal's development during the rest of the fourteenth century was interrupted by several wars with Castile, which earlier had split off from León. Eventually, additional kingdoms—Galicia, Aragon, and Navarra—formed within what is now Spain. Castile was by far the largest and most powerful of these states.

In 1383 Fernando I, the last king of the Afonsine dynasty, died and left the realm in the care of his wife. She intended to rule until their daughter, the wife of the king of Castile, produced a child. Opposing this plan was a popular landholder from southern Portugal—João, the grand master of

the Order of Aviz. João's wealthy religious-military order of knights had a strong army, which he used to expel Fernando's queen.

In response, Castilian soldiers invaded Portugal to protect Castile's claim to the Portuguese throne. In 1385, however, the cortes chose João king of Portugal. King João I, the first ruler of the Aviz dynasty, defeated the Castilian army in the Battle of Aljubarrota.

England—a wealthy trading nation and one of Portugal's best customers—helped the Aviz dynasty to power by sending a unit of English longbowmen into action at Aljubarrota. The Treaty of Windsor, signed in 1386, established a permanent friendship between the two countries. Strengthening this pact was the marriage in 1387 of King João to Phillipa, an English princess.

### PRINCE HENRY THE NAVIGATOR

João and Phillipa had five sons. The oldest, Duarte, succeeded his father to the throne. Another son inherited the title of grand master of the Order of Aviz. A third traveled extensively in Asia and Africa, while a fourth son died in a Moorish prison. Their most celebrated child was Henry

In 1385 at Aljubarrota, Portuguese soldiers under King João I advanced on Castilian troops from Spain. Portugal's success at the Battle of Aljubarrota stopped Castilian military attacks on Portugal for nearly 200 years.

Lisbon's Monument to the Discoveries faces the Atlantic Ocean, which drew the interest of princes and explorers in the 1400s and 1500s.

As a youth, Prince Henry — João I's son — was a serious student of mathematics and astronomy. With this knowledge, he planned many sailing expeditions but went on none himself.

They sailed down the western coast of Africa and by the 1440s had explored the Gambia and Senegal rivers on that continent. These voyages expanded geographical knowledge and gave the Portuguese access to gold, salt, and slaves.

## The Portuguese Empire

While Henry was gathering his team of explorers, Arabs and Italians controlled Europe's trade with Asia. The Arabs collected the Asian goods, which the Italians had the sole right to resell in Europe. Henry believed that he could break that monopoly by sailing around Africa to reach India and the far parts of Asia—a wild notion at the time.

Henry's death in 1460 did not stop Portuguese navigators from continuing their expeditions. In 1488 the Portuguese explorer Bartolomeu Dias rounded the Cape of Good Hope, the southernmost point in

—later known as Prince Henry the Navigator—who achieved fame as a patron of science and exploration.

As a young man, Henry displayed outstanding bravery in 1415, when he captured Ceuta, a Moorish stronghold and trading center in North Africa. After this battle, he retired to Sagres in southwestern Portugal. Henry brought knowledgeable navigators, mapmakers, and mathematicians to his court to improve the science of sailing. The prince was also interested in enlarging his income through the use of the seas.

Henry's brother, the king of Portugal, granted him revenues from the Algarve as a reward for his bravery at Ceuta. These funds helped the prince to finance his school of navigation. Henry's other brothers, who traveled widely, also encouraged many expeditions.

Portuguese seafarers ventured from Lisbon and Sagres, landing on Madeira in 1419 and reaching the Azores in 1427.

Portuguese adventurers charted many sea routes to Asia. Here, Vasco da Gama accepts the greeting of a prince in India, where the explorer landed in 1498.

Africa, to reach the Indian Ocean. Ten years later, his fellow countryman Vasco da Gama landed in India and returned with a cargo worth 60 times the cost of his entire voyage. Da Gama's sea route to eastern Asia enabled Portuguese merchants to directly import valuable spices, precious stones, and other Asian products without having to use Arab or Italian brokers.

In the sixteenth century, Portugal became Europe's leading trading nation and naval power. Its neighbor, Spain, made voyages of conquest to the Western Hemisphere, which Europeans called the New World. To avoid clashes of interest, Pope Alexander VI drew up an agreement that divided new territories between the two Roman Catholic powers. In 1500, when strong winds drove Pedro Álvares Cabral's ship off course, he landed in Brazil, South

The royal mission of Pedro Álvares Cabral was to establish trade agreements with leaders in India, but he did not immediately reach his destination. Heavy Atlantic winds drove Cabral's ships off course, and he landed in Brazil on the eastern coast of South America in 1500.

Afonso de Albuquerque was a major figure in Portugal's activities in Asia. His success in taking territory and in making treaties caused jealousy among Portuguese politicians. In 1515 one of Albuquerque's enemies persuaded the king of Portugal to fire Albuquerque as viceroy of India, and he died there soon after receiving the news of his dismissal from office.

America. The pope's agreement allowed Cabral to claim the new land for Portugal. The rest of the South American continent came under Spanish control.

In Asia the adventurer Afonso de Albuquerque also spread Portuguese authority. In 1510 his forces took Goa, a trading outpost on the western coast of India, and made it the headquarters for Portuguese commercial and missionary activities in Asia. In 1511 he captured Malacca, mainland Asia's large trading station on the Malay Peninsula. He signed treaties with the rulers of several Asian islands to sell their products to the Portuguese, who could then resell the goods in Europe.

Profits from trade brought Portuguese kings vast revenues. Asia supplied valuable spices and silks. Gold, pepper, and slaves were imported from Africa, where Portuguese explorers had established a string of colonies along the western and southern coasts. Many of the slaves were sent to Brazil, where Portuguese planters had set up estates to raise export crops, such as sugarcane and coffee. Portugal—which had few domestic products to sell besides wine, olive oil, cork, and fish—drew most of its income from its overseas colonies.

### THE EMPIRE WEAKENS

As the Portuguese Empire expanded, it needed many sailors and ships to service colonies that stretched from Brazil in South America to Macau on the coast of China. Thousands of men were lost in shipwrecks, died from disease, or were killed in battles with local peoples who did not accept Portuguese authority. By the late 1500s, Portugal's far-flung territories had begun to burden the empire's finances and population.

In addition, Portugal's desire to spread the Roman Catholic faith caused unrest among non-Christian peoples in the new territories, as well as in Portugal itself. The church was trying to convert everyone on the Iberian Peninsula, but particularly Muslims and Jews, to Christianity. These groups had long lived in Portugal, practicing their religions without much interference. The church also wanted to end heresy (opposition to its teachings).

Out of these efforts arose the Portuguese Inquisition, an attempt by the Roman Catholic Church to punish anyone suspected of heresy or non-Christian beliefs. As a result of ruthless measures and harsh judgments, many non-Christians—as well as some Portuguese Christians accused of heresy—were imprisoned, expelled, or executed.

## Spanish Occupation

By the late sixteenth century, Portugal's finances were spread very thinly and royal leadership was weak. For example, King Sebastião, who was fascinated with military exploits, launched an expensive attack on the Moors in North Africa. The disastrous campaign in 1578 cost 9,000 Portuguese lives, including the king's, at the Battle of Alcazarquivir. Following the battle, the dead king's uncle, Henry, succeeded to the Portuguese throne. He died two years later, leaving no direct heirs.

King Philip II of Spain, whose mother had been a member of the Portuguese roy-

Courtesy of Marc C. Wigley

European cannons still overlook Macau, the territory on the coast of China that the Portuguese have run since 1557. Macau offered Portuguese merchants a secure port from which to trade Chinese and European goods.

Belém Tower in Lisbon commemorates the spot from which da Gama and other explorers left Portugal on their sea voyages. The tower's architectural style, called Manueline, features intricate carvings and ornate decoration.

Photo by Dr. Roma Hoff

al family, immediately declared his right to Portugal's crown. Philip also had a strong army to back up his claim. By the end of 1580, Philip had bribed and fought his way to power. The cortes formally recognized him as the new king of Portugal under the name Felipe I.

Portugal, which remained independent under Felipe I, kept its own court system, laws of taxation, and administrators. Spain, however, determined Portugal's foreign policy and drew Portugal into European wars that drained Portugal's treasury. After Felipe I died in 1598, his successors, Felipe II and Felipe III, made even greater demands on Portugal's finances.

Under Spanish rule, Portugal had less money to spend in defense of its Asian trade routes and colonies. Some European customers—the Dutch and the English, for example—avoided Portuguese merchants and began to import goods directly from Asia. The new traders captured many Portuguese ships and possessions and eventually eliminated Portugal as an important trading nation in Asia. This loss made Africa and Brazil even more important to the national economy.

## Independence Regained

In 1640 these problems fostered a revolution against Spanish rule. Portuguese nobles asked João, the duke of Bragança —who had a distant claim to the Portuguese throne—to become the new king. With the help of workers, merchants, and nobles, King João IV freed Portugal of Spanish influence and reestablished the country's independence.

After ending the Spanish occupation, the Portuguese resumed friendly relations with Great Britain (formerly England), which had often been at war with Spain. The Methuen Treaty of 1703 renewed British-Portuguese trade. British cloth and Portuguese wine became common items of exchange between the two countries.

During the reign of João V (1706–1750), Portugal regained much of the prosperity it had lost at the end of the sixteenth century. Again the source of wealth was outside Portugal. Prospectors in Brazil discovered gold in 1692 and found diamonds in 1728. Brazilian agricultural products—coffee, cacao, and sugarcane— also created the fortunes of many Portuguese.

Beginning in 1580, Portugal came under Spanish rule. In 1640 Portuguese nobles invited João, the duke of Bragança, to lead their revolt against Spanish occupation. After their victory, the nobles offered the throne to the duke, who became King João IV at a public ceremony.

Wealthy investors built fashionable new homes in Lisbon and other Portuguese towns, and foreign trade increased. The king used royal revenues to strengthen the army and navy, to construct public and royal buildings, and to improve religious and educational institutions. Because João no longer needed to raise money from nobles and merchants, he stopped calling the cortes into session and governed only with the help of advisers.

João V's son, José I, had little interest in ruling and left this task to his secretary, the Marquês de Pombal. In the mid-eighteenth century, this official discovered that revenues from Brazil, particularly from its shipments of gold, were falling. He reorganized the nation's finances while attempting to regain lost income. With his new authority, the marquês updated Portugal's tax system and improved the country's commercial partnerships.

Under the Marquês de Pombal, Portugal had a flourishing trade in port wine and exported tobacco, sugar, and gold. In 1755, when an earthquake leveled Lisbon, the marquês was able to direct the city's reconstruction on an elaborate scale. In tackling the country's economic problems, however, he made many enemies and imprisoned a number of influential church leaders and merchants. When José I died in 1777, the new monarch dismissed the Marquês de Pombal from office.

## Portugal at War

Struggling economically, Portugal could not afford foreign conflicts and was reluctantly drawn into the European wars of the late 1700s and early 1800s. At this time, the French general Napoleon Bonaparte was trying to conquer Europe, and Portugal allied itself with Britain against

France. In 1807 the Portuguese refused Napoleon's order to arrest all British citizens in the country and to seize their property. In response, the French invaded Portugal, and the Portuguese royal family fled to Brazil. In 1808 British troops landed in Portugal, and by 1811 they had defeated the French. A British officer ruled in the name of the Portuguese monarch.

After the final downfall of Napoleon in 1815, liberal ideas swept through Europe. Many people had endured severe hardships during the years of conflict and wanted better living conditions. In Portugal, unrest and violence broke out among Portuguese who opposed Britain's interference in their country's internal affairs. In 1820 the Portuguese army demanded that the cortes be reassembled. The cortes then wrote a new constitution that limited the monarch's role and that provided for an elected legislature.

João VI, who in 1816 had become king of Portugal while living in Brazil, accepted the terms of the new constitution and returned to his homeland in 1821. He left his heir, Dom Pedro, in charge of Brazil, the wealthiest part of the Portuguese Empire. Preferring to remain in Brazil, Dom Pedro declared the colony's independence and gave up his claim to Portugal's throne in favor of his daughter Maria da Glória.

After João VI died in 1826, his son Dom Miguel tried to take over the kingship. Dom Pedro returned to Portugal to fight for Maria's right to rule, defeating Dom Miguel in battle in 1834. Dom Pedro died soon after his victory, and Dom Miguel was exiled.

During Maria's reign, which ended in 1853, opposing political factions struggled for power in the cortes. Some of these factions wanted to broaden voting rights and to limit royal power. Other groups focused on economic issues, worrying that the costly internal and European wars, which Portugal had financed with large loans, would ruin the nation's economy.

## Changes and Conflicts

In the second half of the nineteenth century, political disputes eased, and two groups—the Regenerators and the Progressists—emerged. The Regenerators wanted to modernize Portugal's economy and to help the nation regain its financial footing. The Progressists, on the other hand, sought to extend voting rights, to educate the population, and to limit the powers of the central government.

Members of both groups came from the same educated, wealthy class. As a result, compromises were friendly, and the two political groups took turns in power. Successive administrations built railways, reorganized the government, and improved higher education.

Portuguese politicians paid little attention, however, to the country's underlying economic problems. The nation had few industries and lacked the money, skilled labor, and raw materials to start them. Portugal's trade depended on re-exporting goods from its colonies. The country's

Independent Picture Service

**Leader of a conservative faction in Portugal, Dom Miguel — an exiled Portuguese prince — tried to take over the kingship in 1826.**

33

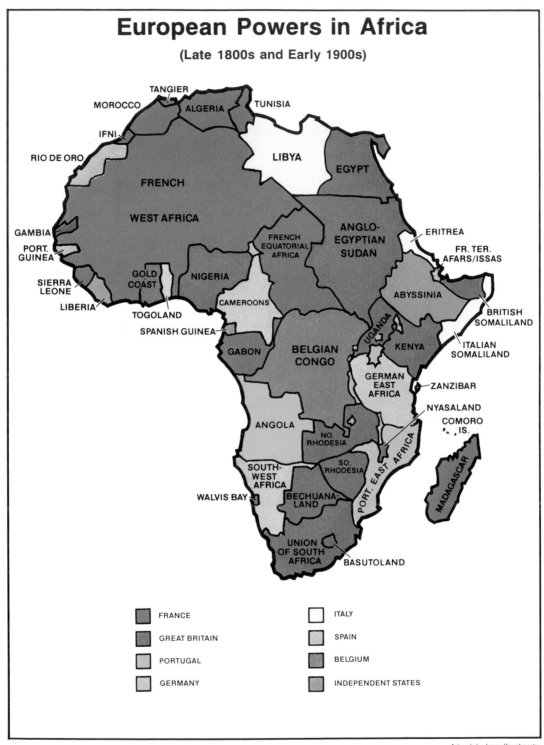

# European Powers in Africa

## (Late 1800s and Early 1900s)

TANGIER
MOROCCO
ALGERIA
TUNISIA
IFNI
RIO DE ORO
LIBYA
EGYPT
FRENCH
WEST AFRICA
GAMBIA
PORT. GUINEA
FRENCH EQUATORIAL AFRICA
ANGLO-EGYPTIAN SUDAN
ERITREA
FR. TER. AFARS/ISSAS
SIERRA LEONE
GOLD COAST
NIGERIA
LIBERIA
CAMEROONS
ABYSSINIA
TOGOLAND
BRITISH SOMALILAND
SPANISH GUINEA
UGANDA
KENYA
ITALIAN SOMALILAND
GABON
BELGIAN CONGO
GERMAN EAST AFRICA
ZANZIBAR
NYASALAND
COMORO IS.
ANGOLA
NO. RHODESIA
SOUTH-WEST AFRICA
SO. RHODESIA
PORT. EAST AFRICA
MADAGASCAR
WALVIS BAY
BECHUANA-LAND
UNION OF SOUTH AFRICA
BASUTOLAND

| | |
|---|---|
| FRANCE | ITALY |
| GREAT BRITAIN | SPAIN |
| PORTUGAL | BELGIUM |
| GERMANY | INDEPENDENT STATES |

Artwork by Larry Kaushansky

By the late 1800s, European powers, including Portugal, had carved the continent of Africa into many colonies. Portugal claimed Portuguese Guinea (now Guinea-Bissau) in West Africa as well as Angola and Portuguese East Africa (now Mozambique) in southern Africa. (Colonial map information taken from *The Anchor Atlas of World History*, 1978.)

traditional exports—wine, olive oil, salt, and cork—did not provide enough money to create new industries. The loss of income from Brazil, which strongly maintained its independence, forced Portugal to borrow large sums of money from foreign countries.

Among Portugal's foreign creditors was Great Britain, which had emerged in the 1800s as the world's most powerful trading nation. When Portuguese and British colonial interests in Africa came into conflict in 1890, Portugal was forced to surrender a large area of southern Africa to Britain. This humiliation angered Portuguese politicians, particularly members of the Republican party, which had formed in the 1870s. This party wanted to make Portugal a republic with elected officials. The Republicans felt that the government of King Carlos I had dishonored the nation by yielding to Britain's demands for African territory.

While this debate raged, Portugal continued to experience economic problems. In addition, the king had begun to ignore the cortes. The Republicans, who wanted greater power for the cortes, supported a military coup (takeover) in 1908. The effort failed, and the royal government responded harshly to the attempt. Violence erupted, and during the bloodshed Carlos I was assassinated. Unrest continued under Carlos's successor, Manuel II, who was unable to form a stable administration. After the king was forced into exile in 1910, the Republicans took over the government.

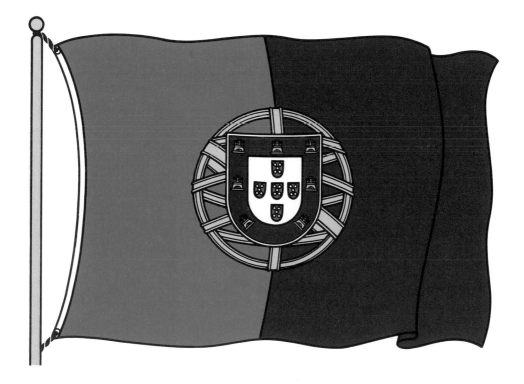

Artwork by Laura Westlund

Dating from 1910, the flag of Portugal is associated with the revolution that occurred in that year. The emblem also has ties to the country's long history. Green symbolizes hope, and red stands for the blood shed during the revolution. The gold device on the flag is an old navigational instrument, recalling Portugal's era of seafaring exploration. The shield is adapted from earlier national flags.

# The New State

Military coups, political assassinations, and indecisive elections occurred as Portugal struggled to establish democracy. Forty cabinets fell during the republic's first 16 years. Economic conditions worsened while internal unrest and global conflicts distracted Portuguese leaders. In 1914 the worldwide conflicts led to the outbreak of World War I, during which Portugal sided with Britain and its allies against Germany. Portuguese leaders believed a German victory would endanger the African colonies that Portugal needed for markets and income.

After Germany's defeat in 1918, Portugal experienced further economic hardships. The government increased taxes and raised prices for food and other goods. These moves did not solve Portugal's financial problems, however, and in 1926 the army seized power. The army chose General António Carmona as president, but the minister of finance (later prime minister), António de Oliveira Salazar, eventually exercised more power. The new government focused on restoring order and reorganizing the economy.

Salazar had complete control of Portugal's finances, and his policies favored the wealthy. In addition to having less money, poor people in Portugal had fewer civil rights. Salazar established a secret police that eliminated all opposition to his government, allowing him to rule as a dictator. Censorship prevented anti-Salazar views from reaching the public. Some political groups, such as the Communist and Socialist parties, were outlawed, and their members were harassed by the secret police.

As these events unfolded in Portugal, Europe again became engulfed in a global

Courtesy of D. G. C. S.

António de Oliveira Salazar ruled Portugal as dictator between 1933 and 1968. A professor of economics, Salazar used his power to address some of Portugal's financial problems, but his methods also curbed public freedoms, weakened social benefits, and eliminated many democratic practices.

Independent Picture Service

Lisbon's Salazar Bridge, one of the longest suspension spans in Europe, was completed in 1966. After Salazar's regime was overthrown, the structure was renamed April 25th Bridge—the date of the revolution in 1974.

Portugal did not take sides during World War II (1939-1945). But Salazar did grant one of the combatants —Britain—the right to build naval and air bases on Portuguese territory in the Azores. Here, a plane from the Royal Air Force flies over the islands before landing.

conflict. Portugal, which did not take sides during World War II (1939-1945), became a safe destination for political and religious refugees fleeing Nazi Germany. In 1943 Britain asked permission to build military bases on the Azores from which to attack German submarines in the Atlantic. The Portuguese government granted the request and also extended similar rights to the United States, which was an ally of Britain.

After the war, many European countries gave up their colonies in Africa and Asia to comply with a declaration by the United Nations (UN), an international agency that had formed in 1945. Portugal joined the UN in 1955 but did not agree to allow its African colonies—which included Guinea-Bissau, Mozambique, and Angola—to become independent. In fact, Salazar's government made these territories provinces of Portugal and gave Portuguese citizenship to the people in them.

Armed resistance to Portugal's policy broke out in Africa in the 1960s and continued throughout the remainder of Salazar's dictatorship. In addition, Asian colonies revolted. India seized the Portuguese overseas territory of Goa on India's western coast in 1961, and Indonesia began to resist Portugal's hold on the island of East Timor in Southeast Asia.

In Angola in the 1960s, Portuguese troops narrowly missed a trap set in a dirt road by Angolan guerrilla fighters.

## Recent Events

In 1968 the aging Salazar had a stroke and left office. Marcello Caetano, who had been a member of Salazar's government, replaced him. The new prime minister tried to introduce economic and political reforms, but Salazar's harsh policies were slow to change. Young officers in the Portuguese army began to press for broader reforms, including more democratic practices. On April 25, 1974, the Armed Forces movement removed Marcello Caetano from power without bloodshed.

The leaders of the revolution dissolved the legislature, enacted economic reforms, and gave legal status to all political parties. To strengthen its power, the new Portuguese government made banks, large farms, and other industries the property of the state. The regime also agreed to give up remaining territories in Africa, and in 1974 and 1975 Guinea-Bissau, Mozambique, and Angola won their independence. Indonesia annexed East Timor in 1976.

Throughout the 1970s and 1980s, Portugal was unable to find lasting political and economic stability. Socialists, Communists, and smaller parties competed for control of the government, forcing frequent elections to be called. No government stayed in power long enough to establish an effective plan for change. Economic problems worsened, as unemployment soared and the foreign debt increased. Workers often were not paid their wages, and strikes were common.

Photo © Tony Arruza

Enthusiastic Portuguese wave banners and shout slogans as they parade down Avenida da Liberdade in Lisbon. The demonstration commemorates the bloodless revolution that occurred on April 25, 1974.

Photo by Dr. Roma Hoff

In the late 1970s, as the country faced growing economic problems, signs still proclaimed the goals of the revolution.

Portuguese workers, such as these winery employees in the Douro River Valley, were hard hit in the early 1980s as rising unemployment, frequent strikes, and a huge foreign debt lowered earnings and endangered benefits.

Photo by Dr. Roma Hoff

Amid these growing difficulties, Portuguese officials opened discussions with the European Community—called the European Union (EU) since 1993. This group, to which most western European countries belong, follows economic policies that benefit all its members. Hoping that membership in the EU might ease its economic hardships, Portugal joined the group in 1986.

Portugal entered the EU as it poorest member. To compete with the other EU countries, the nation had to restructure its economy. The prime minister, Aníbal Cavaco Silva, sold back into private hands the banks, businesses, and farmland that the government had acquired in the mid-1970s. These measures met with resistance from groups that favored the revolution's

In 1986, in Lisbon's ornate, sixteenth-century Hieronymite Monastery, Portuguese president Mário Soares *(left)* signed the papers that officially made Portugal a member of the European Community (now the European Union).

original policies. Nevertheless, Cavaco Silva and his ruling Social Democratic party, which had a majority in the legislature, were able to pass the reforms.

Portugal receives money each year from the European Regional Development Fund which was created to modernize the infrastructures of the EU's poorest members. The country must also reorganize its economy if it hopes to join the monetary union the EU has proposed for the twenty-first century. The union would mean that all EU member-countries would have the same currency to ease trade and travel.

A new government came to power in 1995. The Socialist party won the general elections in October, and Antonio Guterres replaced Cavaco Silva as prime minister. The new government's challenge is to make Portugal ready to become a stable member of the EU by continuing to modernize the

country's infrastructure and industry and by returning more public companies to private hands.

## Government

Portugal is a republic, and political power is held by an elected legislature and an elected president. The country's constitution was written in 1976 but has been revised several times. The document guarantees certain civil rights, such as freedom of speech and of the press. All citizens over the age of 18 can vote.

The Portuguese parliament, which is called the Assembly of the Republic, has one house of 230 members, who make and approve the nation's laws. The delegates serve four-year terms. A system of shared representation, in which even small parties have a chance to win seats, gives the legislature a broad range of political views.

The president serves a five-year term and appoints the prime minister, who heads a cabinet (the Council of Ministers) that designs government policies. At the beginning of a new term in office, the prime minister and cabinet submit their program to parliament. If the legislature does not reject the program, the new government is confirmed in office.

Portugal's judicial system has many different courts. District and appeals courts operate at the local level, and a supreme court hears cases that the local courts have failed to decide. Separate courts also exist for the military and for administrative agencies. A nine-member tribunal reviews new laws to make sure they do not conflict with the national constitution.

Mainland Portugal is divided into 18 administrative districts, each of which elects its own governor and legislature to make local decisions. The Madeiras and the Azores became internally autonomous (self-ruling) areas in 1976 and 1980, respectively. Macau, an overseas dependency, is a small outpost on the coast of China that is scheduled to be returned to Chinese control in 1999.

Courtesy of D. G. C. S.

Aníbal Cavaco Silva served two consecutive terms as prime minister. He reversed economic decisions made in the first decade after the revolution by returning some government-run businesses to private ownership and decreasing the amount of farmland under state control. His actions set the pace for Portugal's integration into the EU.

The Portuguese parliament, or Assembly of the Republic, meets in a former monastery that was rebuilt in the 1800s to house the legislature.

Independent Picture Service

41

Portuguese in rural and urban areas, such as this woman in Coimbra, often carry goods on their heads. Portugal maintains many traditional ways, which give the country a reputation of being less modern than some other European nations.

Photo by Susan Guernsey

# 3) The People

Including the people of the Azores and the Madeiras, Portugal has nearly 10 million inhabitants. Sixty-six percent of the nation's citizens live in rural areas. Compared to other European countries, this is a very large percentage.

Throughout the nineteenth and twentieth centuries, many Portuguese emigrated to Brazil and to Portugal's African colonies. Some people left to seek better conditions in other parts of Europe or in the United States. Thus, despite a high birthrate in these centuries, the Portuguese population grew slowly. Since the mid-1970s, however, the number of Portuguese emigrants has declined.

The Portuguese were once mainly of Iberian background, but intermarriage with conquering, colonizing, and visiting peoples has changed this ancestry. In northern Portugal, the language and the local place-names reveal ties to ancient Celts, Suevi, and Visigoths. Moorish links are stronger in central and southern Portugal, where Arab and Berber groups lived.

The ancestry of people on the Azores—which were uninhabited until Portuguese explorers landed there in the fifteenth century—is entirely Portuguese. The population of the Madeiras has a mixed African and Portuguese heritage. Brazilian influences have come to Portugal mainly through books, newspapers, and films, rather than through immigration. The arrival of Portuguese-speaking Africans called *retornados* has introduced aspects of African culture to the Portuguese.

## Way of Life

An important geographical division within Portugal has affected the country's history and attitudes. The Tejo River separates the north, which resisted conquest, from the south, which had frequent contact with outsiders. This distinction still exists to some extent, giving the northerners a reputation for being conservative and the southerners a more worldly outlook. Similarly, townspeople near the sea have usually had more liberal views than Portuguese who live inland.

Portugal's many villages and towns often show evidence of past conquerors. For example, Celtic hilltop villages, called *castros,* dominate the north, while the whitewashed cottages of the south reflect North African architecture. In central Portugal lie the well-planned Roman cities of Braga, Évora, and Coimbra.

Courtesy of Portuguese National Tourist Office

**Living conditions have improved in Portugal in the last few years as political stability has allowed health care and educational services to be upgraded. These young Portuguese can look forward to better chances for schooling and jobs than their parents had.**

As Portugal's economy grows and improves, jobs and other opportunities draw more rural people to the cities. The expansion of urban areas, where developers have built new port facilities and industries, may eventually end rural dominance.

## Health

Medical facilities are not as well developed in Portugal as they are in other European countries. A national health service that distributes free medical care started in 1979. In 1990 private health care became an option to publicly funded health services. About 28,800 doctors serve the entire country. In most rural areas, patients rely on a combination of folk medicine and modern practices. Older women in northern villages, for example, use herbs to cure colds and other ailments.

Since the 1974 revolution, the government has spent more money on education and construction, and the number of medical professionals and health clinics has increased. Portuguese people have an average life expectancy of 75 years, a typical figure among western European nations. In the area of infant mortality, Portugal has improved. The mortality rate has decreased from 15 deaths in every 1,000 live births in 1991 to 8.6 deaths per 1,000 in 1995—a figure only slightly higher than the rest of western Europe.

## Education and Language

Portugal's educational system is among the poorest in Europe. Rural areas lack facilities, and many children leave school at a young age to help their families earn a living. Illiteracy has long been a problem,

Independent Picture Service

Women gather around a community well in a Portuguese village. Although some homes do not have in-house plumbing, most of the population has access to clean, safe drinking water.

Black-caped students pass in front of one of the old buildings at the University of Coimbra. For a time, students associated the black gowns with the Salazar regime and refused to wear them.

and 15 percent of the population cannot read or write (down from 29 percent in 1970). The government made education a high priority in the 1990s, devoting 12 percent of the national budget to this area.

All Portuguese children between the ages of 6 and 15 must attend elementary school. Many students do not pass their final examinations on the first try and must retake them before entering secondary school. This level of education is not compulsory and can last from one to five years. About 40 percent of the students who begin secondary schooling finish their studies. Some secondary schools provide job training, while others prepare graduates for higher education.

Portugal has 12 universities and 14 technical schools, all of which are run by the government. About 120,000 students attend postsecondary institutions, the oldest of which is the University of Coimbra.

Founded in Lisbon in 1290, the school moved in the 1500s to a royal palace in Coimbra that once belonged to King João III.

Portuguese is one of the Romance languages, a group that also includes Spanish, French, Italian, and Romanian. All of these tongues are rooted in the ordinary Latin that the Romans spoke about 2,000 years ago. Portuguese has retained some grammatical forms that no longer exist in the other Romance tongues. Educated Portuguese can easily read Portuguese texts from the thirteenth century.

The Portuguese spoken on the Iberian Peninsula is closely related to the Spanish language used in Spain. Nevertheless, the two languages are distinct. In fact, Portuguese people and Spaniards usually cannot understand each other in everyday conversation. Dialects of Portuguese include Galician, which is spoken by people in northwestern Spain, and Brazilian.

In the town of Estremoz in the central Alentejo, a skilled carver carefully sculpts a piece of locally quarried white marble.

## The Arts

The Portuguese royal family and the Roman Catholic Church supported most early painting, architecture, and music in Portugal. Portuguese artisans translated the work of foreign craftspeople into a local style. Painting on panels, for example, came from Flanders (now northern Belgium) in the fifteenth century. Nuno Gonçalves became a master of this technique, producing a six-paneled panorama of the court of Afonso V for a church in Lisbon. Talented mapmakers drew charts of outstanding cartographic quality in the same period.

In later centuries, other forms of artistic expression became more prominent than painting. In the sixteenth century, for example, a distinctive method of sculpting and building called Manueline developed. Named for King Manuel I, this style appeared in doorways, window frames, pillars, and monuments. Manueline artists let their imaginations roam freely, using spiraling columns, seafaring motifs, angels, knights, and animals to create a busy, flowing arrangement of images and shapes.

Modern Portuguese craftspeople still practice many folk arts, including basketry, lace making, pottery, and linen weaving.

The Convent of Christ in Tomar has a famous window carved in the Manueline style. Beneath a cross are vertical columns covered with marine imagery, including ropes, seaweed, coral, and fishnets.

Courtesy of Catherine F. Rodgers

*Azulejos* (ceramic tiles) have long been used to decorate the interiors and exteriors of public and private buildings. The tiles often display the geometric patterns and bright colors of Moorish art.

Church leaders and Portuguese monarchs fostered the development of music by providing places for the performance of instrumental and choral pieces. Troubadours (poet-musicians) sang in the early

Photo by Dr. Roma Hoff

Accompanied by guitarists, a *fadista,* or female singer of *fado* music, performs in a Portuguese club. In Coimbra, fado involves only male singers.

47

royal courts, and kings later actively supported opera. Church schools offered musical training, especially for organists.

The folk music of Portugal remains widely popular. Lively dance tunes and sad, wistful compositions are both common. After dinner, some Portuguese visit houses or clubs to hear *fado* music, in which a guitarist accompanies a singer. Fado music is somber, and the lyrics tell of tragic loss or past glories.

## Literature

Portugal has a long literary tradition, although not many of the country's writings are known to outsiders. Nationalist writers composed many epic poems and patriotic songs after Portugal gained its independence in the mid-twelfth century. Two of Portugal's early kings, Afonso III and Dinis, were accomplished writers and troubadours. More than 2,000 songs survive from the thirteenth and fourteenth cen-

Independent Picture Service

Each region of Portugal has its own folk dances. These dancers are from northern Portugal, where famous dances include the *vira* and the *malhão*.

turies. Fernão Lopes chronicled the lives of Portuguese kings during the late fourteenth and early fifteenth centuries. In the

Courtesy of D. G. C. S.

A drawing of Luíz Vaz de Camões shows him crowned with a laurel wreath to signify his premier place among Portuguese poets. Born in about 1525 into a poor, noble family, the young Camões left his homeland to find adventure and wealth in Africa and Asia. While overseas, he wrote *Os Lusíadas* (The Lusiads), an epic story of brave Portuguese heroes and their exceptional deeds. It became the great classic of Portuguese literature, inspiring poets and writers for many centuries after Camões's death in 1580.

same period, Gil Vicente achieved fame as a writer of comedies and religious dramas.

The most famous writer of the sixteenth century, and perhaps the nation's greatest author, was Luíz Vaz de Camões. His long work, *Os Lusíadas* (The Lusiads), was published in 1572 and became a European classic. In epic form, the book details the voyages of the Portuguese explorer Vasco da Gama. More than an example of Portuguese heroic literature, however, *Os Lusíadas* brought new words into the language and broadened the scope of verse forms. Camões also wrote stirring sonnets and philosophical plays that describe the ideals of love and the pitfalls of destiny.

The publication of Camões's work coincided with Spain's takeover of the Portuguese throne. Many Portuguese authors from the sixteenth to the eighteenth centuries wrote in Castilian Spanish rather than in Portuguese. Another work of the period—*Lettres portugaises* (Portuguese Letters)—first appeared in French. Enormously popular when they were published in 1669, the letters chronicled an affair between a Portuguese nun and a French nobleman.

The poet João de Almeida Garrett and the historian and novelist Alexandre Herculano led a rebirth of Portuguese literature in the nineteenth century. Writing in Portuguese, they used their country's folklore and history in their works. The novels of Camilo Castelo Branco describe social habits in northern Portugal. Hope and despair alternate in the verse of the Azorean poet Antero Tarquínio de Quental.

In the early twentieth century, Portuguese literature exhibited the spirit of *saudade,* a sense of longing or nostalgia for the past. Contributing to this style was Fernando Pessoa, who gained a reputation as a critical, solitary, and intensely nationalistic poet during this period.

Portuguese writers suffered during the Salazar dictatorship, which heavily censored all published and broadcast material. One of the regime's last bans was placed

Camilo Castelo Branco (1825-1890) wrote a large number of novels. They revealed his keen interest in rural life and in small-town views on love, birth, and religion.

The twentieth-century poet Fernando Pessoa published under many names, each of which had a different writing style and social background. Pessoa felt this approach to his work broadened the modes of expression available to him.

Photo by Dr. Roma Hoff

Coimbra's old Roman Catholic cathedral draws the faithful to services every day.

Photo by Dr. Roma Hoff

A mother and her two children approach the shrine at Fátima, where believers hear masses and attend vigils that celebrate the anniversary of a vision of the Virgin Mary.

on *Novas cartas portuguesas* (New Portuguese Letters), a collection of essays, letters, and poetry written by three women named Maria. Inspired by the earlier *Lettres portugaises,* the work caused the "three Marias" to be tried and convicted on charges of obscenity. After the revolution in 1974, the new government issued the authors a pardon and allowed their book to be published.

## Religion and Festivals

Most Portuguese are Roman Catholic, and about one-third of the people regularly attend services—a high proportion compared to other European countries. The Portuguese constitution guarantees freedom of religion, and small communities of Jews, Muslims, and Protestants also practice their faiths. For most of the nation's

citizens, the church is an important part of daily life. In rural areas, Roman Catholic clergy frequently participate in local governmental, educational, and social activities.

Catholicism is the basis of many Portuguese festivals, in which processions, bullfights, folk dancing, and fireworks mark the feast days of local and national saints. From May to October, nearly 500,000 Portuguese go to a shrine at Fátima, where in 1917 three children claimed to have seen a vision of Mary, the mother of Jesus. The pilgrims, who often arrive at the shrine on their knees to show their devotion, leave gifts as further tokens of esteem.

The Festa dos Tabuleiros in Tomar is celebrated to give thanks for the harvest. At this gathering, young Portuguese women parade through the streets balancing tall *tabuleiros* (wicker baskets) on their heads. The baskets contain careful arrangements of bread interwoven with flowers and blades of wheat. After the procession, the people enjoy four days of folk dancing and fireworks.

## Food

Meals shared by the family are a key part of Portuguese daily life. A light breakfast is followed in the afternoon by a three-course main meal, which usually consists of soup, fish, and meat or vegetables. In the middle of the evening, the Portuguese eat a moderate supper.

Spices are important in most Portuguese recipes, and the variety of seasonings results from centuries of seafaring expeditions. Pepper, cinnamon, and curry powder, for example, came to Portugal from India and are now staples in Portuguese cooking. Chili pepper, garlic, and coriander are also popular. The spiciest foods are prepared in the Azores and the Madeiras, where sailors often traded foreign spices for fresh fruit and vegetables.

A family enjoys its midday meal, which includes fish, bread, vegetables, and wine.

Photo by Betty Groskin

*Caldo verde* (green soup) is made from a tender, deep green cabbage. Thick chunks of *chouriço* or *lingüiça* (spiced sausages), as well as potatoes and onions, fortify this national dish.

Photo © Tony Arruza

A young resident of Olhão, a town on the southern coast, grills sardines on a small barbecue.

Portuguese cuisine is famous for its filling stews and hearty soups, including the national dish called *caldo verde* (green soup). Made from a special type of cabbage, this soup also contains potatoes, onions, garlic, and thin slices of spiced sausage, such as *lingüiça* or *chouriço*.

Portugal's seafaring traditions have made fish, especially *bacalhau* (dried, salted cod), a common offering. Declines in the annual catch have forced Portuguese cooks to buy some of their bacalhau from Norway. Seafood stews, called *caldeiradas,* often contain whatever the local fishermen have hauled in that day, along with tomatoes, garlic, and onions. Vendors grill plump sardines on streetside barbecues during the sardine season, which lasts from May to October.

## Sports and Recreation

The Portuguese engage in a variety of sports either as participants or spectators. Soccer, called *futebol,* dominates the sports scene, and thousands of fans pack the coun-

try's stadiums. Professional teams from Lisbon and Oporto have wide followings, but the country also supports semiprofessional and amateur clubs. Oporto's team won the European Champions Cup in 1987.

Portuguese bullfighting is a major attraction and differs from Spanish bullfighting. In Spain, the bull's death is part of the spectacle. In Portugal, the animal is killed after the bullfight is over. Most bullfighting in Portugal is done on horseback, and the well-trained horses and skilled riders usually come from the Lisbon area.

Car racing has become an established sport, and the annual Grand Prix of Portugal held in September attracts a large crowd. Racing is so popular with the Portuguese that a grand prix is even held in Macau, the tiny territory that Portugal will maintain in China until 1999.

Born in 1958, Rosa Mota has become one of the world's best long-distance runners since beginning her marathon career in the early 1980s. After winning several European races, she triumphed in the Olympic marathon in 1988, completing the 26-mile run in 2 hours, 25 minutes, and 40 seconds.

*Futebol,* or Portuguese soccer, draws thousands of fans when the national teams play.

Although not noted for Olympic medalists, Portugal triumphed in 1984 and 1988, when Carlos Lopes and Rosa Mota respectively won marathons in the summer games. Portugal's facilities for golf, tennis, skiing, and other sports cluster in cities and national parks throughout the country. In mountainous areas, people have opportunities to fish, hike, and ride horses amid beautiful scenery.

The streets of downtown Macau are blocked off for the annual grand prix auto race. Run in November, the event involves formula-three cars, which have smaller engines, lower weights, and narrower wheel bases than formula-one cars have.

Courtesy of Transinsular, S. A.

Originating in Lisbon, a huge cargo ship arrives at Funchal, the capital of the Madeiras, with a load of cars and other heavy goods. Trade is a major part of the Portuguese economy.

# 4) The Economy

Until the 1970s, Portugal earned most of its foreign income from trading its own agricultural products and from reselling imports. Since then the country has developed many industries, which now make more money than farming does. In the 1990s, factories employed twice as many people as agriculture and earned five times as much for the country. Portugal, however, remains a poor country, with a 1996 average income per person of $4,390—45 percent lower than the average per capita income for other EU countries.

Although Portugal, along with the rest of Europe, is recovering from an economic recession that occurred in the early 1990s,

it has many opportunities for economic improvement. A member of the EU since 1986, the country has been modernizing its industries to compete successfully against other businesses in the EU market. To help Portugal do this, the EU has provided funds, advice, and training.

The Portuguese government is using the money to upgrade agriculture, industry, and services, such as the telephone and transportation networks. These economic activities have traditionally needed many manual laborers. After modernization is in place, high unemployment might result, because machines will replace some forms of hand labor.

54

## Industry

Throughout most of the twentieth century, Portuguese governments did little to expand the manufacturing sector, which employs about 23 percent of the labor force. Companies remained small and were clustered in the north, where road and rail networks are poor. After Portugal joined the EU, however, these conditions began to change. Foreign and domestic developers built manufacturing centers in Lisbon, Setúbal, Braga, Aveiro, and Oporto.

The north's textile and shoe industries are modernizing, shifting from the production of cheap goods to the making of high-quality clothing and computer-designed footwear. Ceramics businesses in the same region have switched from crafting pottery for local markets to manufacturing expensive decorator tiles for export.

Photo by Melanie Friend/The Hutchison Library

**A worker at a clothing factory in Coimbra pauses beside a large bolt of fabric.**

Photo © Tony Arruza

Leather shoes crowd a window in Lisbon and range in price from 700 to 4,800 escudos (roughly $5 to $30). Footwear is one of the country's leading manufactured items. Manufacturers made more than 90 billion pairs of shoes in the mid-1990s, most of which are exported to Europe and the United States.

Large, wooden wine casks line the walls of a storage center in Colares, the main town in a small wine region on the Atlantic coast. The red wines of Colares are made from thick-skinned, dark blue Ramisco grapes, which grow only in the sandy soil of this region. In recent years, some vineyard owners have sold their land to housing developers. As a result, the Ramisco grape variety is in danger of losing its habitat.

Independent Picture Service

The port wine industry—long a mainstay of trade with Britain—is also looking to the future. New grape varieties are slowly expanding the country's wine selections. Yet the traditional quality of the nation's port and Madeira still attracts European buyers. Portugal furnishes about 80 percent of the world's cork, which is used to make bottle stoppers, life preservers, insulation, and soundproofing material. Cork scraps are ground up and made into floor tiles and bulletin boards.

Portugal's largest cities have heavy industries, including steel mills, oil refineries, and shipbuilding complexes. After 1974 all these businesses were nationalized (changed from private to state ownership), but they will again return to private hands. In addition to these industries, Portugal has cement factories, ironworks, chemical plants, and canneries for fruits, vegetables, and fish.

## Agriculture

About 11.5 percent of the Portuguese people farm the land, more than 50 percent of which is under cultivation. Northern farms are very small, usually covering five acres. In this mountainous region, farmers use traditional methods and grow just enough food to feed their families. The rocky terrain and farmers' traditional methods have slowed the introduction of modern equipment in the northern provinces.

In the south, however, most agricultural holdings are larger than 200 acres, and many estates are still owned by the government. Reforms have allowed some of these big farms to be returned to private hands. Modern machinery, fertilizers, and other innovations are gradually replacing older methods of growing fruits and vegetables.

The most important food crops are wheat, oats, rye, barley, rice, and potatoes. Grapevines thrive on terraces that have been cut into the steep hillsides flanking the Douro River. Fruit from these vines is made into port wine or sometimes vinhos verdes. Farmers on Madeira raise another type of grapevine for their wine. The Azores provide tropical fruits, and mainland orchards yield apples, pears, peaches, and oranges for export. Tomatoes have become more important, because they are processed into tomato paste, which other European countries buy in large quantities. In southern Portugal, workers gather the nuts from almond trees and the fruit from olive trees. The olives are crushed to make olive oil.

Independent Picture Service

Using poles, workers shake olives from trees onto a canvas before pressing the fruit into olive oil. To harvest the olives for eating, workers must pick them off the branches one by one.

Laborers bend from the waist to plant rice seedlings in a flooded field. The grain thrives best in the western coastal plains, where water and sunshine are plentiful.

Courtesy of Minneapolis Public Library and Information Center

On a hillside in the Douro Valley, a grape picker places the bluish purple fruit in his basket. Harvesting is often accomplished by hand, especially where steep, terraced fields make modern machinery difficult to use.

Livestock plays an important role in Portugal's rural economy, especially in the north, where herds of dairy and beef cattle are common. Some farmers also raise sheep and goats and use donkeys for transportation. Pigs thrive throughout the country and provide meat and hides.

## Fishing

With its ready access to the sea, Portugal has long been a fishing nation. This industry is also undergoing change, as fish stocks drop and as old-fashioned boats become less suitable for commercial fishing. Nevertheless, fishing villages dot the Atlantic coast, especially where sandy beaches offer safe landings.

Portuguese fishermen sail in heavy, high-prowed vessels that lack motors and are often difficult to maneuver in the Atlantic's strong tides and currents. After launching, the boat heads straight out to sea, trailing a line that is firmly anchored on shore. After two or three miles, the boat turns and sails parallel to the coast for about a half mile as fishermen on board slowly drop a long net. The boat then turns back toward the beach, dragging another cable that is attached to the net.

The fishermen have set up a rectangular-shaped trap. Upon landing, they haul the large net to shore. This difficult work, along with Atlantic gales and fish shortages, makes fishing a dangerous and sometimes disappointing occupation.

Sardines, mackerel, hake, and flounder are among the various types of fish caught. About half of the sardine haul—which is brought into Setúbal, Matozinhos, and other ports—is canned for export. Fishermen from the Algarve specialize in intercepting the annual run of tuna heading for the Mediterranean. Every year a fleet leaves Lisbon for North American waters to fish for cod.

## Forestry and Mining

Replanting and careful management have kept about one-third of Portugal forested. In fact, the most common forest products—cork and olives—are harvested without harming the trees.

Cork trees grow mostly in the southern part of the country, extending over about 500,000 acres in the Alentejo and the Algarve. The bark on these trees must build up for at least 20 years before it can be stripped. After the first stripping, the bark slowly grows back. Cork may be removed legally from a tree only once every 11 years. The quality of cork improves with the age of the tree.

The climate throughout Portugal is suitable for cultivating olive trees, but most groves exist in the east. Workers press oil out of the flesh and seeds of olives. The nation's pine forests provide turpentine and resin, as well as softwood for building purposes.

Mining is a small industry in Portugal. The country has developed only a few of its minerals, including iron, tin, and wolframite. A hard metal, wolframite is used to strengthen electrical equipment and

Photo by Carlos Freire/The Hutchison Library

Boxes of freshly caught fish line the wharf at Sines, a fishing hub on the Atlantic coast.

steel. Large deposits of iron and tin are worked in northern Portugal. Wolframite, the only mineral exported in large quantities, comes chiefly from east central Portugal, near Castelo Branco.

## Transportation and Energy

Portugal has spent a significant portion of the EU's development funds to improve the nation's transportation network. Major roads run mainly north and south along the Atlantic coast. Since Portugal joined the EU and expanded commercial ties with Spain, the east-west routes—some of Portugal's poorest—have become important to overland trade.

Portugal maintains about 20,000 miles of roads and about 3,000 miles of railroads. Roughly 85 percent of the roads are paved. Except for the track between Lisbon and Oporto, the railways are old and slow, but they serve most of the country. In cities, people use cars, buses, streetcars, and subways to get around. In rural areas, horses, mules, and donkeys are still common forms of transportation.

The government owns and operates the nation's airline, TAP Air Portugal, which links Portugal with other parts of Europe, as well as with several African countries. Lisbon, Oporto, and Faro have international airports, and regional airfields carry domestic traffic. The sea is another means of transportation to the rest of the European continent. The main ports of Lisbon and Oporto receive heavy traffic. Most of Lisbon's docks handle international cargo while Oporto's are usually filled with regional goods.

One of the obstacles to industrialization in the 1970s was the lack of cheap energy sources to power factories. Since then the Portuguese government has built hydroelectric plants on the Tejo and Douro rivers. These stations now supply 46 percent of the nation's power, with the remainder coming from coal and oil. Portugal is heavily dependent on foreign energy, importing electricity and oil from its EU

Workers pile curved strips of cork onto carts for transport to a factory. Portugal's cork oak trees are among the nation's most valuable forestry resources, providing most of the world's cork.

A cement carrier brings its cargo past Lisbon's historic Praça do Comércio, a huge plaza along the Tejo River.

Portugal refines imported oil at several sites along the Atlantic coast.

partners. In rural areas, wood is still a common fuel in homes.

## Tourism and Trade

With its sunny climate, Portugal has become a popular tourist site. The Algarve and the cities of Lisbon and Oporto draw most of the visitors, who brought in about $4.8 billion in foreign revenue in 1994—more than double the income from the early 1990s. The tourism industry may offer opportunities to the many farmers and laborers who could lose their jobs as Portugal restructures and modernizes its economy.

Vacationers flock to the white beaches of the Algarve, from which travelers can explore some of the country's historical sites. Roman ruins exist near Coimbra, and a handsome palace and castle in Sintra are a short journey from Lisbon. The tropical

Rising on an island in the Tejo River, Almourol Castle has a romantic history that attracts many foreign visitors.

The casino, beaches, fine restaurants, and first-class hotels of Estoril make this Atlantic resort a major tourist destination.

heat and colorful vegetation of Madeira attract tourists to this volcanic island, where hiking and swimming are popular activities.

Portugal's economy has long depended on trade, both to make money and to supply essential goods. Before 1974 the country relied on its overseas colonies to provide cheap raw materials and a guaranteed market for Portuguese manufactured items. Now, without its colonies, Portugal conducts most of its trade with fellow EU members. Nearly all its energy and about half its food come from the EU.

France and Germany rank high among Portugal's leading customers and suppliers. Spain is now Portugal's chief supplier of goods. Britain also provides many im-

ports to the Portuguese market. The United States, which does not belong to the EU, is Portugal's largest buyer of cork.

Besides cork, Portugal's exports include canned fish, wine, olive oil, tomato paste, textiles, resin, turpentine, and wolframite. The nation imports machinery, heavy industrial equipment, steel, petroleum products, food, and coal.

## The Future

Although nostalgic about their past, the Portuguese have much to look forward to in the coming decades. Long isolated from European affairs, the country has plunged into a massive market by joining the EU. This move, although of benefit to the nation in the long run, will cause substantial changes in trade, agriculture, and industry.

After many years of unstable governments, Portugal appears to have a lasting administration in place whose goal is to help the country move into the twenty-first century. The challenges of this goal may cause the nation's workers to suffer some short-term problems, such as unemployment and high prices.

As the poorest EU country, however, Portugal needs to compete with its fellow members at every level. Large amounts of EU funds will help the nation to modernize, and expanding trade with Spain and other EU states is expected to give Portuguese industries a needed boost. The country's prospects seem strong, if the Portuguese work force and government can seize these new opportunities for growth.

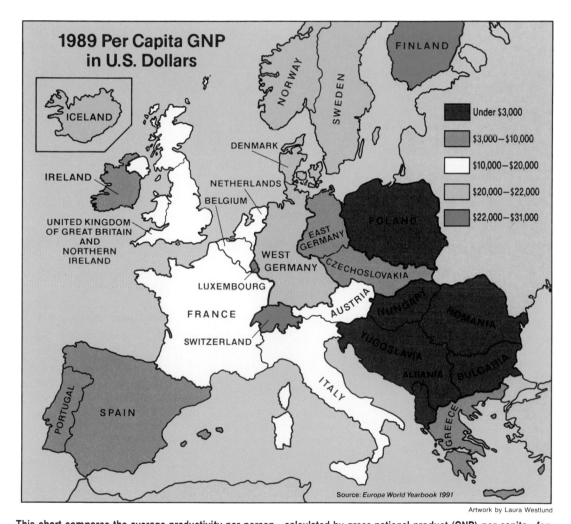

**1989 Per Capita GNP in U.S. Dollars**

| | |
|---|---|
| ■ | Under $3,000 |
| ▨ | $3,000–$10,000 |
| □ | $10,000–$20,000 |
| ▨ | $20,000–$22,000 |
| ▨ | $22,000–$31,000 |

Source: *Europa World Yearbook 1991*

Artwork by Laura Westlund

This chart compares the average productivity per person—calculated by gross national product (GNP) per capita—for 26 European countries. The GNP is the value of all goods and services produced by a country in a year. To arrive at the GNP per capita, each nation's total GNP is divided by its population. The resulting dollar amounts indicate one measure of the standard of living in each country. In 1989 Portugal's GNP per capita was $4,269. By the mid-1990s, the GNP was $7,890 (compared to Europe's average of $11,870). Although Portugal's economy has grown since it joined the European Union, it is still one of the poorest nations in the EU.

# Index